Pebble® Plus

Baby Animals

A Baby Polar Bear Story

by Martha E. H. Rustad

Consulting Editor: Gail Saunders-Smith, PhD

CAPSTONE PRESS
a capstone imprint

Shh! A mother polar bear peeks out from her den. Her twin cubs snuggle close inside the den, drinking milk and growing bigger.

3

Spring has come.

Let's go outside. Blink!

Bright sun shines on

the cubs' white world.

Yawn! Tired cubs rest close

to their mother.

Even spring is cold

in the Arctic.

Playful cubs tumble in the snow. Padded feet and long claws help them walk on snow and ice.

Time to leave the den for good!

The cubs follow mom across

the snowy tundra.

She looks for open water.

She's hungry for a meal.

The cubs watch mom hunt
seals at holes in the ice.
Stay still. Don't move. Pounce!
Yum! Mom shares a taste
with her cubs.

One cub slips into
the icy water!
Yikes! Mom will help
her cub out.

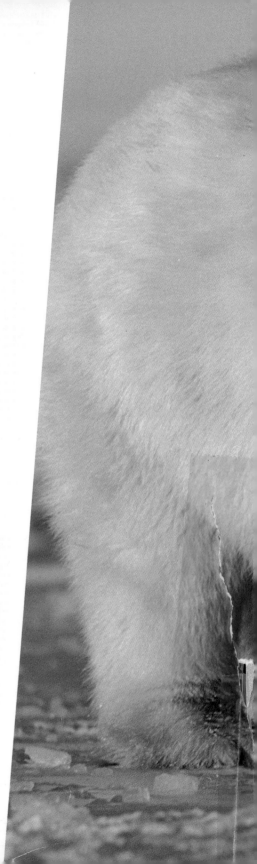

Paddle, paddle—keep on
swimming! Cubs learn
to swim from their mother.
A layer of blubber keeps
them warm in icy water.

What's over there?

Mom is always on

the lookout for danger.

Her cubs stay with her

until they're two or three.

Good-bye, mom! Good-bye, sister! The polar bear is off on his own. He'll swim, hunt, and find a mate in his Arctic home.

Glossary

Arctic—the areas surrounding the North Pole

blubber—a thick layer of fat under the skin of some animals; blubber keeps animals warm

den—a hole in the ground or snow where a wild animal lives; female polar bears dig dens in snow banks

mate—a male or female partner of a pair of animals

tundra—a cold area of northern Europe, Asia, and North America where trees do not grow; the soil under the ground in the tundra is permanently frozen

Read More

Kalman, Bobbie. *Baby Polar Bears.* It's Fun to Learn about Baby Animals. New York: Crabtree, 2011.

Royston, Angela. *Polar Bears and Their Homes.* The Big Picture. Mankato, Minn.: Capstone Press, 2011.

Thomson, Sarah L. *Where Do Polar Bears Live?* Let's Read and Find Out Science. New York: Collins, 2010.

Internet Sites

FactHound offers a safe, fun way to find Internet sites related to this book. All of the sites on FactHound have been researched by our staff.

Here's all you do:

Visit *www.facthound.com*

Type in this code: 9781429660631

Check out projects, games and lots more at
www.capstonekids.com

Pebble Plus is published by Capstone Press,
1710 Roe Crest Drive, North Mankato, Minnesota 56003.
www.capstonepub.com

Books published by Capstone Press are manufactured with paper
containing at least 10 percent post-consumer waste.

Library of Congress Cataloging-in-Publication Data
Rustad, Martha E. H. (Martha Elizabeth Hillman), 1975–
 A baby polar bear story / by Martha E. H. Rustad.
  p. cm.—(Pebble plus. Baby animals)
 Includes bibliographical references and index.
 ISBN 978-1-4296-6063-1 (library binding)
 ISBN 978-1-4296-7093-7 (paperback)
 1. Polar bear—Infancy—Juvenile literature. 2. Bear cubs—Juvenile literature. I. Title. II. Series.
 QL737.C27R88 2012
 599.786'139—dc22   2010053927

Summary: Full-color photographs and simple text describe how polar bear cubs grow up.

Editorial Credits
Erika L. Shores, editor; Ashlee Suker, designer; Svetlana Zhurkin, media researcher; Laura Manthe, production specialist

Photo Credits
Alamy/Steven J. Kazlowski, 5, 14–15, 21
Ardea/M. Watson, 3
Dreamstime/Outdoorsman, 1, 8–9, 10–11
Getty Images/The Image Bank/Joseph Van Os, 6–7; Stone/Daniel J. Cox, 18–19
Minden Pictures/Rob Reijnen, 13; Suzi Eszterhas, cover
Photolibrary/Dan Guravich, 16–17

**Capstone Press thanks Suzann G. Speckman, PhD, and Thomas J. Evans, with the
Marine Mammals Management department of the U.S. Fish and Wildlife Service,
for their assistance in reviewing this book.**

The author dedicates this book to her son Markus Johan Rustad.

Note to Parents and Teachers

The Baby Animals series supports national science standards related to life science.
This book describes and illustrates polar bear cubs. The images support early readers in
understanding the text. The repetition of words and phrases helps early readers learn
new words. This book also introduces early readers to subject-specific vocabulary words,
which are defined in the Glossary section. Early readers may need assistance to read
some words and to use the Table of Contents, Glossary, Read More, Internet Sites, and
Index sections of the book.

Printed in the United States of America in North Mankato, Minnesota.
112011   006464R

Index

Word Count: 200
Grade: 1
Early-Intervention Level: 18